THEO VON TAANE

FUNCRAFT
HAPPY NEW YEAR TO ALL MINECRAFT FANS!
(UNOFFICIAL NOTEBOOK)

NOT AN OFFICIAL MINECRAFT PRODUCT. NOT APPROVED BY OR ASSOCIATED WITH MOJANG.

Bibliografische Information der Deutschen Nationalbibliothek:
Die Deutsche Nationalbibliothek verzeichnet diese Publikation in der Deutschen Nationalbibliografie; detaillierte bibliografische Daten sind im Internet über http://dnb.dnb.de abrufbar.

© *2017 Theo von Taane; 2. Auflage*

Texte und Illustrationen: **Theo von Taane**

Herstellung und Verlag: BoD – Books on Demand, Norderstedt

ISBN: 9783743159976

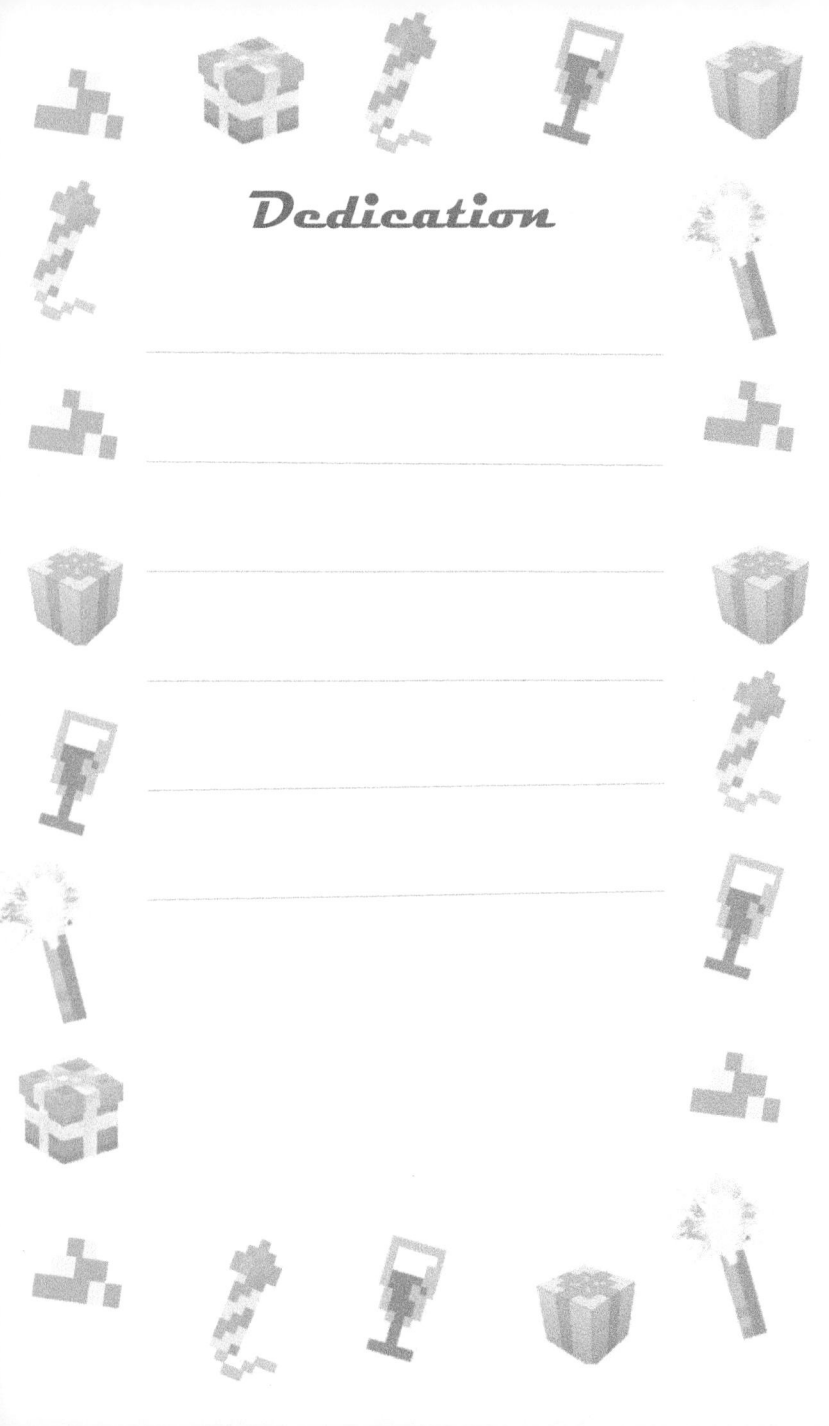

Dedication

More books of Theo von Taane

book	ISBN / order nr.
FUNCRAFT - The unofficial Math Coloring Book: Minecraft Minis	9783743137523
FUNCRAFT - The unofficial Math Coloring Book: Superheroes in Minecraft Skin	9783743138025
FUNCRAFT - The best unofficial Math Coloring Book for Minecraft Fans	9783743138933
FUNCRAFT - The unofficial Notebook (quad paper) for Minecraft Fans	9783743148734
FUNCRAFT - The best unofficial Notebook (ruled paper) for Minecraft Fans	9783743154186
FUNCRAFT - Merry Christmas to all Minecraft Fans! (unofficial Notebook)	9783743149151
FUNCRAFT - Happy New Year to all Minecraft Fans! (unofficial Notebook)	9783743159976
Password Logbook for Minecraft Fans	9783743163386
Pokefun - The unofficial Notebook (Team Red) for Pokemon GO Fans	9783743159983
Pokefun - The unofficial Notebook (Team Yellow) for Pokemon GO Fans	9783743159990
Pokefun - The unofficial Notebook (Team Blue) for Pokemon GO Fans	9783743160002
Pokefun - The best unofficial Notebook for Pokemon GO Fans	9783743160040
Majestic Flowers and Butterflies - Adult Coloring Book	9783739227085
Football 2 in 1 Tacticboard and Training Workbook	9783734749605
Badminton 2 in 1 Tacticboard and Training Workbook	9783734749643
Baseball 2 in 1 Tacticboard and Training Workbook	9783734749650
Basketball 2 in 1 Tacticboard and Training Workbook	9783734749681
Bowling 2 in 1 Tacticboard and Training Workbook	9783734749698
Cricket 2 in 1 Tacticboard and Training Workbook	9783734749711
Ice Hockey 2 in 1 Tacticboard and Training Workbook	9783734749728
Fencing 2 in 1 Tacticboard and Training Workbook	9783734749735
Field Hockey 2 in 1 Tacticboard and Training Workbook	9783734749810
Football (Soccer) 2 in 1 Tacticboard and Training Workbook	9783734749827
Futsal 2 in 1 Tacticboard and Training Workbook	9783734749834
Handball 2 in 1 Tacticboard and Training Workbook	9783734749841
Lacrosse Women 2 in 1 Tacticboard and Training Workbook	9783734749858
Lacrosse Men 2 in 1 Tacticboard and Training Workbook	9783734749865
Netball 2 in 1 Tacticboard and Training Workbook	9783734749872
Rugby 2 in 1 Tacticboard and Training Workbook	9783734749889
Chess 2 in 1 Tacticboard and Training Workbook	9783734749896
Squash 2 in 1 Tacticboard and Training Workbook	9783734749902
Tennis 2 in 1 Tacticboard and Training Workbook	9783734749919
Table Tennis 2 in 1 Tacticboard and Training Workbook	9783734749926
Volleyball 2 in 1 Tacticboard and Training Workbook	9783734749933
Water Polo 2 in 1 Tacticboard and Training Workbook	9783734749940

...futher titles available and in preparation.